Runwright.Net Company
New York, NY
Visit the website at http://runwright.net

First Edition: July 2013

Wright, Karen.
Growing Up Wright: What it's like to have the best family in the world / Karen Wright. – 3rd ed.

ISBN 978-1-304-14531-4
1. Memories 2. Childhood 3. Jamaica

Printed in the United States of America

Growing Up Wright

What It's Like To Have
The Best Family In The World

Karen Wright

For my parents,
Lorna and Leroy Wright,
who love me unconditionally,
and for my brother, Mark Wright,
who prayed for a little sister.

First Prayer

I wasn't there for it, but I hear that my existence all began with a prayer.

My brother, Mark, was about three years old at the time. My dad was in the United States of America, studying at Central Connecticut State College, now University. Even though his four-year-long degree program was almost finished, my Mom and Mark had not adjusted to being without Daddy full time and they counted the days until he would return, days marked by the letters he would write home consistently, reminding them he loved them and sharing his foreign experiences so they could be a part of each other's lives even if they were temporarily separated by an ocean and a sea.

As the time for Daddy's return drew closer and Mark realized the family would once again reunite, his dreams for an even bigger family became stronger.

And as Christian parents often teach their children, Mommy encouraged Mark to talk to God about his dreams and make his requests known to Him. Because if you want something, shouldn't you ask The Person who can give it to you?

I wasn't there to witness it but I've heard this story so many times, if I squint my eyes enough and gaze into the distance, I think I can see that little three year old boy, kneeling by his bedside, asking God to bring his Daddy home safely and when his Daddy comes home, can he also bring not just new toys or new clothes or a brand new T.V, but can he please bring a baby sister with him?

So after graduation, my Dad returned to Jamaica to join his family, and my parents decided not to stand in the way of a little boy's prayer being answered.

And about a year later, I was born.

First Memories

They say your memories start becoming long term around age five and one of my first memories is of my fifth birthday. This does not bode well for parents who spend so much time and money planning outrageous parties for babies who are too young to appreciate and will never retain any memories of the event. These days, Photoshop make it appallingly easy to construct "memories" of made-up events. (Note to parents, save the resources for the after-five years.)

For my fifth birthday, my parents took me to Hope Gardens in Kingston to celebrate. I distinctly remember the bright red ribbons that adorned my hair that was not quite long enough to make ponytails. By this time, Mummy had expertly mastered the art of grooming the short hair so my hair would have been expertly coiffed and decorated with the red ribbons.

I wore a beautiful sundress, I am sure. I don't remember the dress but there were so many other beautiful sundresses in what would gradually unfold as my future, that the details of the one I wore on my birthday escapes me. What I do remember is standing in the car, right on the little hump that runs down the middle of the car, so I could put my hands on the back of driver and passenger seats. From that position, I could stand close to my parents and chat excitedly about what I would see and what I couldn't wait to experience based on what my parents had told me to prepare for the day.

It was 1981. There were no seat belt laws in Jamaica. Most cars didn't have seat belts. More so, the child restraint was, even more comfortably, my mom's right arm as she slung it over my dad's shoulder to keep me from jerking forward if the car stopped suddenly.

My older brother, Mark, sat in the back seat so if I fell backwards, he would catch me.

This setup has formed the basis of my whole life. I have never doubted whether my family would be there to support me. They have not always agreed with my decisions but they allowed me the room to make my own way and chart my own course, with their blessings, and always

with their arms ready to catch me if things didn't go as I had planned.
I remember seeing beautiful flowers in the Botanical Gardens and interesting animals in the zoo – a monkey eating peanuts was my favorite, perhaps because he reminded me of a battery-operated, acrobatic, toy monkey I had at home. After Hope Gardens, we probably drove to see my aunt Pam, my father's sister who lives in Kingston. We didn't make many trips to Kingston that didn't include going to see her.
Over the years, I have forgotten many of the details about the day. But I remember standing in the car as we travelled the country roads on our way to the town, my parents and brother listening to me chat excitedly about what I was going to do and how at five years old today, I am finally a big girl now. I remember pressing my chest on my mother's arm when I got a little tired. And like I did on most car trips that lasted longer than twenty minutes, I remember finally being more than a little tired, sitting beside my brother on the back seat and putting my head in his lap for the nap that would likely last the rest

of the journey. I remember being confident that my family would keep me safe and when I woke up, everything would still be great.

For the Love of Books

The Williams family is united in its passion for tennis. Tiger Woods' father took him to the golf course as a baby so he could gain enough exposure to the sport and become the greatest golfer of his time. One of the greatest gifts my family has given me is the love of books.

Each person in my family manifests this love in their own unique way. My brother, who has met many books he would rather leave unopened, will, however, spend many hours poring over a book that gives details of the inner workings of anything mechanical. From him, I have learned the ability to teach one's self almost anything.

As a child, I remember Mark's favorite book was a large tan colored hardcover with a red spine. "Science Topics", it was called. He read that book everyday, focusing on one thing and then another, giving it his undivided attention until he understood it completely, then moving on.

At odd moments, he would search the house for odds and ends and perform his own experiments that borrowed from, but did not mirror the ideas in the book. Mark was the first scientist I ever knew and he inspired me to be the same.

As children, we shared a room, his bed on one side, mine on the other and as every kid with an older sibling knows, whatever the older sibling does seems way more exciting than anything you could think of on your own. In my case, this was doubly so since my brother made things I had never seen before.

We lived in the country parish of St Elizabeth, in a close community where your visitors were usually family members or close friends who you had known your entire lives and so either had unrestricted access to walk into your home unannounced or who could call your name as soon as they turned into your yard so you would tell them to come on in. Or, if you happened to be in the backyard and were out of earshot, one of your next-door neighbors would call to you that this person or that was in the front yard looking for you. We had a system better than any newfangled surveillance system.

Notwithstanding, when my brother was about twelve years old, he designed a doorbell from a couple AA batteries, an old flashlight bulb and the speaker from a junk radio that was lying around our house. I remember being so impressed; it was as though my brother was Thomas Edison himself.

Mark read Physics book like they were New York Times Bestsellers. Later, I would read those same books in school without deriving the same amount of joy. Self-taught science is truly my brother's passion.

My father is the consummate mathematician and where he hesitates to read biographies of other mathematicians or fictional works with titles that sound like math topics but actually have nothing to do with math (I did not immediately realize that The Life of Pi is NOT about that magical number 3.1429…), what my father does read is book after book after book about Mathematics itself. He reads examples of problems. He reads alternative ways to teach Math topics. And when he reads, he works problems out so there are pages and pages and pages of problems in various stages of being solved because when he has gotten to a certain point, there is no need to write the steps to get to the final answer because that time is better spent moving on to the next problem.

In college, I found that I tackle Math problems in the same way. The means, not the end, is what concerns me most.

As a lecturer at the Bethlehem Teachers College, Daddy taught future teachers how to teach Math. In Jamaica, primary school teachers have to be comfortable teaching all the subjects to their students. So my father would have teacher trainees with limited mathematical skills and in whom he had the daunting task of instilling not just an understanding of the concepts they would teach but also a passion they could pass on to their students so they could in turn love the subject. It was a challenge he rose to year after year.

As I grew up, I had several opportunities to witness my dad passing on this gift to his students. One evening when I was just a little girl, I sat in the back of his class, reading or doing a puzzle while I waited on my dad to be finished with his class. I remember the problems like it was yesterday. He was teaching his students how to solve quadratic equations and one student had decided she was never going to be good at this and she decided to raise her hand and tell my dad about her revelation. He didn't skip a beat. When she said, "Mr. Wright, I can't do math. I am never going to learn how to solve these equations," he replied immediately.

"Yes, you will and that's why we are going to stop and start again and go through every step. We won't move on until you understand everything." And he erased the solution and started writing the steps again.

That night, when we went home, he read through the textbook and made some notes, perhaps about what the students struggled with and how he could tackle it. Then he went to the bookcase we kept in the passage and pulled down some other textbooks that presented alternate ways of tackling quadratic equations. Then he went to the box of his notebooks that he had kept from his college days in the United States. Finally, I

saw him pull out the books from Cambridge. Those were the big guns!
I wasn't there for the follow-up class but all his students passed the class that semester. Somewhere, that student had to have realized that what she thought was her revelation was indeed not the end of her story.

My mother is the quintessential reader-writer-poet. She was my first teacher. With her being a primary school teacher when I was born, I started going to school with her perhaps as soon as I was potty trained. I don't remember my first day or year at school, perhaps because I started before I was five years old. What I do have is the first uniform that I ever wore and it is so small it has only three buttons – one for the top, one for the waist and one for the skirt. It hangs in the closet in my parents' house as a reminder that you are never too young to start being educated. My mom taught the sixth grade and although I didn't get to her class officially until I was almost nine years old she always knew what we were doing in school so she reviewed my work with me in the afternoons when we came home from school and then she taught me the other things she wanted me to know.

A lot of these “other things” came from the books she chose for me to read. My mom also doubled as the school librarian so I had an almost unrestricted access to the wealth of books that our small but adequate library possessed. I borrowed volume after volume of the encyclopedia, Nancy Drew, Hardy Boys, The Bobbsey Twins and Paddington Tales. I learned to read while we waited for the Royal Rose bus or for Daddy to come pick us up. In the evening when we’d finished homework and chores, we read as we relaxed. Later, I learned to read and watch TV simultaneously so I could get the best of both worlds.

My early love for books has never waned. As a child, I devoured whatever printed words appeared in front of me. I think it has even inspired me to choose foreign films so I could read the subtitles.

I read my share of Hans Christian Andersen stories and Grimm Fairy Tales as well as Aesop's fables. But the books that have shaped my development perhaps more than any others have been the books that my parents kept in that passage in the middle of our house. It was the treasure chest of information not readily available to other kids my age. Here, they kept the textbooks from their college experiences, books that fed my seemingly unquenchable thirst for words, books that taught me the words adults knew, so I could speak the way adults do. To hear a sentence like this uttered by a child nowadays might cause you to conjure up images of wildly inappropriate words, curse words that would make a sailor blush but that is so far from my intent. What I mean is that my parents had a very poetic and formal way of speaking with their colleagues. They talked about politics and education and social conditions and even the humdrum of the news in a way that amazed me. I heard my dad use words that sounded long and impressive and I wanted to know how he learned words like panache and debonair and became comfortable enough to use them in everyday situations. Those were not words I could find in the small dictionary I carried around in my book bag so I realized I needed to read more of the things they read so I could also learn to speak the way they did.

Even as a child, I knew that when I was older, I would want to be just like them. So I read the newspaper. I read my father's collection of short stories from his Connecticut State College freshman English classes. I read my mother's textbooks on teaching Language Arts to elementary school students from her own classes as a teacher trainee at Shortwood Teachers College.

I read and I read and I read.

I read the Greek Mythology text my brother brought home from high school. I read newspaper articles, even if only to find the name of the presidents and prime ministers of every country (a project Mummy suggested for me when I was about eight years old and at which I worked diligently for years. This project just wouldn't work now with the Internet at our fingertips).

I read the back of cereal boxes. I read sample essays and paragraphs in technical writing textbooks. I read Guide magazines for inspiring stories about Seventh-day Adventist children. I sent away for every free book advertised on the television or in the back of magazines. I started my own library with the numerous books my parents bought me and a copy of John Steinbeck's *The Red Pony* which one of my father's colleagues sent me as a gift.

Today, I have a novel, a newspaper and a small journal in my handbag. Although I also carry around my laptop, extra reading material is never far away. Because one never knows when one might have a golden opportunity to indulge one's true passion and just read.

Education for ALL AGEs

I don't remember the first time I went to Seaview All Age School. Again, my memories of my life don't extend back that far. I might have been a few months or a couple years old. You see, my mother, Mrs. Lorna Patricia Wright was a teacher there, my older brother, Mark Wright was a student there and my father, Mr. Leroy Wright, who was a lecturer at Bethlehem Teachers College would drive them to school and pick them up on his way to and from work, so he was also there twice a day. With the rest of my family already connected with Seaview, all I had to do was get old enough to attend. So I don't know how old I was when I was added to the school register at Seaview but I know I was really young. My first uniform hangs in my closet today as a reminder of how far I've come. That first uniform was so small that it only had 3 buttons - one on the top, one on the waist and one on the skirt. My own experiences there really embodied the name- Seaview ALL AGE school.

I didn't attend the basic school (kindergarten)

across the street. That would have been a safety hazard as I was always trying to cross the street to be back with my mom at the 'big school' as they called it. So I started grade 1 under the tutelage of Ms. Josette Bent, progressed to grade 2 where Ms. Winsome Bent taught me. At the time, it must have been confusing for some people to have two teachers in the school named Ms. Bent so we called one Ms. J. Bent and the other Ms. Bent, that is, until she got married, became Mrs. McCarthy, and made things easier for us. In grade 3, I learned from Mrs. Gloria Wellington and by the time I got to grade 4, the teachers had rotated so I had Mrs. McCarthy again. I only did a few months in grade 4 as the students who were preparing to take exams in January moved into grade 6A, where my mother taught the scholarship prep class.

Since I had started school early, I was only 8 years old when I started grade 6 so I stayed in the class for 2 years, just waiting until I was old enough - you had to have already turned 10 years old when you sat the exams in January. During that time, I learned the preparation books almost by rote, because I was doing the exercises during class, and in the evening at the extra lesson classes that my mom taught after the regular school day ended and again at home where my parents made sure I did my homework. You have no excuse to not do homework when your mother is your teacher. I benefitted so much from that experience but it wasn't without its challenges because I was a full time student.

At school I had to remind myself not to call her Mummy when I asked a question in class. We were always the last children to leave school - well except for Kirk and Ava Foster. Their mom was Mrs. Foster, the school principal and they lived at the cottage on the school premises. They were always at school. The children of the teachers were not allowed to be mediocre- we had to be examples, living out the principles being taught at school. But then there were the benefits, too many to count.

I was a small child and when the bigger students would play games, they would protect me. In baseball games and netball games, I was always the 'jack-a-man' - I could play on either side so if it was baseball, whether I wanted to field or bat, I could play. I didn't have to worry about leaving my lunch money at home or of I forgot my homework. I didn't have to remember to tell my parents about school events. And I didn't have to worry about my report cards because my parents always knew how I was doing in school - there was no surprise there.

When I was a student at Seaview, the student body was divided into 3 houses - Stephenson, Soares and Ebanks houses. We lined up for assembly and devotion in our houses, we were assigned duties in our houses and we competed at sports events in our houses. At our morning assembly, we were inspected to ensure that we had clean clothes, that our hands and face, hair and general appearance were clean and neat. All infractions were recorded and the house would lose points.

Weeping willow trees lined the long driveway leading up to Seaview school and the houses would be assigned to sweep the debris that littered the asphalt driveway and settled around the trees.

The students were also assigned to clean the bathrooms that were in the back of the schoolyard. We used brooms made from bushes collected from the little hill close to the school to do our duties and when we were done, we would be inspected to get points.

At the end of the school year, the points were tallied and a winning house would be named. I remember my house, Stephenson, winning most years but that might just have been me choosing to keep only pleasant memories.

For most of the school year, from Monday to Thursday, we were served school lunch from our school canteen. The first cook I remember was Ms. Cookie. She would roll out long stretches of dough on the counter and cut them to make dumplings. As early as 10:00 a.m. when we were at recess, we could pass by and see Ms. Cookie in her white apron stirring that big pot of dumplings cooking on the fireplace in front of the canteen. I don't think Ms. Cookie was her real name but what the students knew about her testified to her supreme cooking skills. She would make a delicious chicken stew to serve with the rice and dumplings and those boys would devour as many dumplings as she could prepare. The canteen was a tiny room but the food that came from that canteen was like Jesus feeding the five thousand- a multitude was fed and after all were satisfied, there were still 12 basketfuls remaining.

The environment at Seaview was one of constant learning - the teachers all had a curriculum that they taught us from - Mathematics and English Language, Science, Social Studies and Religious Education - but we learned so much more about general knowledge and about how to make our way and succeed in the world.

Our days would start with devotion where children who didn't attend church had the opportunity to learn about God and those who did attend church had an opportunity to reinforce what they had learned. The principal or another teacher would explain a scripture passage so the Bible became real to us. Other times, they would offer encouragement and inspiration, which showed us how to see the world as much bigger than where we were at the time.

We had a school library where we were encouraged to choose books for extracurricular reading. The informal reading clubs that developed because of our love for the Nancy Drew and Hardy Boys books instilled our love for reading, which in turn enforced our love for learning. The book mobile would visit the school each term and a few of the older students would get to participate in choosing the books - that taught us how to make responsible that would impact others on a large scale.

On Friday mornings, in our classes we did General Knowledge, which taught us how to pay attention to current affairs and the news. We learned various arts and crafts and all the students, both boys and girls learned to sew- how to embroider and appliqué. We learned how to make art with simple household items like carving patterns in a potato to create a stamp and dye clothes. We had a local 4H club where all of us as students got an opportunity to showcase

our handiwork, but there were also ways to show the usefulness of what we had done.
I remember the year my mom had all the students embroider their names on a piece of white cotton fabric and she used it to make a cushion cover. As the Jamaican idiom goes, we learned how to "turn we hand and mek fashion. We didn't know it at the time but we were being prepared for adulthood, we were being prepared to be mothers and fathers, teachers and lawyers and doctors and engineers, farmers and fishermen; we were being taught to be contributing members of our social and professional circles. Those lessons have followed us through our lives. We've incorporated the resourcefulness and creativity to form our careers and enrich our lives and the lives of those around us. Seaview ALL AGE School - preparing students to be better in ALL the AGEs and stages of our lives.

Summertime

The beauty of my parents being teachers meant that when we had school holidays, they also had school holidays so we were never passed off to babysitters. When I got older, I went to summer camp a few times but the best summer memories I have are still of the months I spent at home with my mom.

The fun things kids learned in school on Fridays when the attendance was too low for the teacher to start a new topic, formed the base for our summer activities. My mom had been the coordinator of the school 4-H club, which taught arts and crafts. Also, she had grown up without many material possessions to call her own and poverty teaches resourcefulness so she taught us cool ways to use things.

This was my introduction to recycling. We saved toothpaste caps and the covers from soda bottles and used them to make collages. We collected fresh flowers, pressed them between the pages of heavy books and used them to make bookmarkers or decorate homemade greeting cards. Mummy taught us to embroider and do crochet, creating countless tea towels and tray-cloths that employed both art forms.

At school, the boys in her class loved learning to sew, many of them coming from homes where their parents didn't think boys needed to learn these skills. On our couch, Mummy even displayed a couple white cushions on which her students had embroidered their names. It was useable art.

My mom had a Singer sewing machine and she liked to sew. She would take these yards and yards of fabric and fashion dresses and skirts and shorts for me. She would alter the clothes I got from well-meaning relatives who hadn't seen me in years and so had no idea of how big or small I really was. I remember getting a dress from a cousin who lived in the United States and who was a few years older than me. I remember Mummy measuring me and measuring the dress and then going to work redesigning it - pulling the seams and refashioning it into a jumper and then later into a pair of shorts. My mom hasn't yet showed a collection in New York's Fashion

Week but that fact doesn't make her any less a fashion designer.

And now when I read biographies of famous designers, I realize I was my mother's muse. Oscar de la Renta had Scarlett Johansson, Givenchy had Audrey Hepburn, and my mom had me.

She made a few khaki shirts for my brother but most of his clothes were tailor-made or his uniforms bought from the supply store but most of my uniforms were made with her tender loving care, hands expertly cutting and basting and stitching and pinning darts for the many fittings we would do right in her bedroom.

Sometime in the beginning of the summer, we would make a trip to Neil's Enterprise, also known as Hurry-Hurry and buy the Dacron and Cotton for my uniforms. When I was still at Seaview, it was a navy blue tunic and sky blue blouse; at Hampton, it was a sky-blue tunic and white blouse. She knew the patterns but she would usually open the seams of one of my old uniforms and use them as a guide to make the new uniforms just a little wider and a little longer. She would sew on the waistbands; she would use chalk to mark the buttonholes and then make them with zigzag stitches sewn very close together. She would call me after each major step for a fitting, sometimes telling me to be careful because there were still pins holding up some part of it. I saw my outfits grow - from ideas inspired by a pretty dress hanging in a store window or from a picture in a magazine, to choosing from the bolts of cloth in the fabric store through to a work of art hanging on my body and when the buttons were ready to be sewn on or the hem to be completed by hand, she would call me to help so I would have some part in making my own clothes.

When I was about to start high school at Hampton, we attended an orientation where they brought out samples of uniforms that were acceptable and those that were not. There were very strict rules about the color of the uniform, the width of the waistband, the number of buttons overall and how many could be placed on the waistband, the placement of the pockets, how many rows of stitches could be used to border the pockets and placket of the tunic. There were rules about how long or short the sleeves could be. The rules were endless and my mom didn't want me to have a hassle so she bought the material at the approved store and took it to a seamstress to have my uniforms made.

That year, we missed out on the fun of making those uniforms so she made me other clothes instead.

Lessons learnt, the next summer, we were back to our tradition. Even when she was busier than usual and I had the occasional uniform made by another dressmaker, she still supplemented my clothes by making me something. One weekend, I would see her open the bed-trunk and take out a piece of fabric and she would announce, "I am going to make you a skirt."

When I was old enough to start wearing some of her clothes, I tried on one of her jackets one day and she liked the way it looked on me. That weekend, she made me my first jacket suit for church. It was an aquamarine jacket and skirt suit. It fit me so well, I tried to wear it every Sabbath. I might have gone to church just for the opportunity to wear it.

Puzzles

Everybody in our family loves puzzles of some kind. Daddy loves crossword puzzle books. I remember being so impressed with how smart my Daddy was because the crossword puzzles seemed impossible.

Mummy would do the big crossword puzzle in the newspaper and I remember as a child trying to understand just how crossword puzzles worked. How did you fit all those clues inside those little boxes? Over the years, I have pursued the crossword puzzle challenge too. Years and years of practice have made me still an amateur but someday I hope to be as good as they are.

My brother, Mark, loves jigsaw puzzles, like Grandpa did, and he can sit for hours at the table covered by hundred of jigsaw pieces, all the pieces alike but nothing fits. Seems like a lot of work to make a picture but it's the process, not just the result that matters. Mark 's passion for putting things back together was always evident though. When we were younger, he was most happy when he could pull a radio apart and put it back together and get it to work. My dad had an old Phillips radio in the house, with a wooden case and a fabric cover on the front panel. It had been in the house for years and everybody knew it didn't work. One day, Mark decided he was going to check it out and he pulled it to pieces. There were little red bits here and little blue bits there and wires everywhere. There weren't any two pieces of that radio that were connected when he completed the demo. But then he started to work on it. He must have been the proud owner of his first soldering kit by this time and he joined and pulled apart and joined again, pieces that had long bid a sad goodbye to each other. I don't know how long it took him but the radio worked. And then one evening, when we had all settled into the living room, as casually as though we had just acquired a new electronic item, Mark walked over and turned the dial and music flowed from that rejuvenated wooden box. I think Daddy was impressed. I know I was!

Home on the Farm

I grew up in Southfield, a rural community on the south coast of St. Elizabeth, the parish known as the breadbasket of Jamaica. Most of the income of the parish comes from some kind of agricultural pursuit. Driving through any of the districts, in Southfield and in the neighboring communities, Seaview, Junction, Pedro Plains, you are likely to see houses away from the street and large vegetable gardens in front of them. Our current house is no exception.

Although my parents are both very involved teachers, they have always had one crop or another in a garden somewhere. The house where we grew up had a lawn in the small front yard but the backyard was always green with either Irish potatoes or corn or cauliflower or sweet peppers or red peas or tomatoes and there was always a little herb garden with a mint bush, a few roots of scallion and a few thyme bushes. The herb garden was constant. It wasn't until I moved to the United States that I realized how much I miss having a herb garden. Because growing up in any house in St Elizabeth meant there were always fresh herbs to pick to season the rice and the chicken pots. And if for some reason you didn't have your own herb garden (as unlikely as that might be), your neighbors garden was as available to you as if it were your own, because nobody minded the people who lived next to them coming by to break off a few sprigs of thyme or pulling up half a root of scallion. The trick to harvesting the scallion would be to separate the root and only pull up one side so the other side could remain in the soil to continue growing until it was needed for the next meal.

My dad loves having animals around and he continues to raise goats, cows and chickens for recreation more than for economic gain. We didn't have a big enough backyard for the crops and the animals so he built a goat pen at the end of our lot and in the morning we would take the goats out and tether them to iron stakes we would drive in the ground. There was a lot of unused government land around beyond the housing scheme so we could leave the goats to graze without worrying whether they would be safe. In the evening, we would return and pull up the stakes and lead the goats back home to the pen until the next morning.

When there was a bad storm, if we had a ewe who had just given birth, we would bring the goat and the kids into the kitchen until the storm was passed. Live and let live!

When I was about eight years old, I got my own goat from Grandma. I was sick one day and staying with her instead of being in school. I had been reading "Sprat Morrison", a beautiful Jamaican novel about a boy who lives in the city but goes to visit family in the country and makes friends with a goat named Mischief. That day, I too made friends with one of Grandma's goats, a white kid with black patches all over her body. At the end of the day when she told me I could take the goat home with me, it was not hard to decide on what her name would be. Mark also got a goat that day, the brown and black sister of my goat and so we decided that for their names to match, mine would be called Mischief and his would be called Naughty. Helping with the animals now became even more of a joy and we spent many hours just watching those goats grow up and having baby kids of their own. It was like becoming a proud grandparent.

The number of goats on hand fluctuated greatly. Kids were always being born and unfortunately dying. There was a man who lived on the other side of the big playfield behind our house and he had huge, fierce dogs behind his fence. Every now and then, his dogs would get loose and we would lose one of our animals. Sometimes we would go on long trips and get back home so late we couldn't go to take the goats home and they would be at the mercy of the elements. Most times, nothing untoward happened and they would be fine when we went to move them in the morning.

Every now and then, they weren't. It pained my dad's heart every time he had to bury one of his animals but it was a part of the circle of animal life on the farm.

Whenever there was a big party, my dad would butcher one of these goats and we would have a big pot of *manish* water and a huge curried goat stew. These parties often happened at Christmas or New Year when we went to the Grandma Kez's house in Manchester to meet up with the rest of the family or a few times when the party came to our house in Southfield. Early in the morning, Daddy would take one of his own young fat rams, or if there were none mature enough, he would buy a ram for this purpose. He would use a rope to hoist it to the big Poinciana tree in our backyard and slit the goat's throat. He would be careful to move all his other animals from the vicinity so they wouldn't see what was going on and start their own Animal Farm riot. The ram would twist and jerk, spewing blood all around for a few minutes. Then, when the blood had drained sufficiently, Daddy would start dressing the animal. Ironically, dressing the animal meant removing its skin, an intricate process done with a sharp knife, the blade paring the skin from the tender muscle underneath. He would slit the underside of the animal and remove the belly, pouring it into a huge basin. Someone would come to collect it to clean the tripe. I remember a neighbor, Miss Reiner, doing this a few times, taking the long intestines and squeezing the undigested food out, using a stick to turn the narrow tubes inside out to wash them in water over and over until they were clean enough to eat. My mom would cut these up, to make tripe and beans later, and for soup stock for the manish water now. The goat head would also be removed and parts of it chopped up for the soup pot. Then my dad would chop the meat for the stew. No part of that goat was wasted. Someone always took the goatskin, I am not sure why but I think they used it to make drums, in homage of our African heritage.

The chickens were another story altogether. Sometime around 1990, we became chicken farmers too. Daddy built a pen in the backyard, behind the Poinciana tree and bought a hundred baby chicks. The pen was close enough that he could keep an eye constantly trained on them but far enough away from the house that we didn't hear the chicks chirping all through the night. They ate constantly.

By this time, Mark was an electrician and he ran some wires so they had light and they could eat throughout the night. Daddy bought bag feed and threw it in the coop and placed a couple water dispensers that kept the water constantly replenished. He crushed tablets and put in their water to protect them from disease. For every hundred chicks he bought, a few of them wouldn't make it. As they moved about in the coop, the weak ones would be attacked and when my dad went to feed them, he would periodically have to remove one after another that didn't survive. Over the course of an eight-week cycle, a few would die and maybe eighty-five to ninety would make it to the harvest. First, there was a huge cauldron of water boiling on an open fire. Daddy would go into the coop and take a chicken and with a very sharp knife, slit the neck and remove the head. The headless chicken would flap its wings and jostle about for a while. If it wasn't restrained, it would try to run around. There is an idiom that talks about running around like a chicken without its head. I saw firsthand what that meant.

Restraining the chicken was something to be done in moderation though, because if the chicken flapped around too much, its wing might get broken and nobody wants to buy chickens with bloody, broken wings. One or two in a batch was bad but not terrible. If most of the chickens were similarly defective, we would not be able to sell them. My dad was very good at butchering the chickens and holding them securely. We didn't have many of those chickens with broken wings but the ones that did, we usually kept for our own kitchen.

All my family members got involved in plucking chickens. We would hold the freshly killed chickens by the feet and plunge them into the cauldron of boiling water. When they were sufficiently doused, we could pull the white feathers off easily. If the feathers were hard to remove, it meant the skin was not warm enough so we would dip it in the boiling water again as often as needed to remove all the feathers and long hairs that covered the chicken's body. Then it was time to hold the chicken by the neck and get the feet hot so we could peel off the skin on the claws. Some of the chickens were easier to skin than others; some you could just get enough skin to grip and pull and it would separate leaving the nails behind. Others require more peeling and then you had to cut the tips off. When this was finished, we would put them in another pan of cold fresh water to rinse off the scum and someone would slit the bird to remove the entrails and the crop and clean it up. All the chicken livers were collected in a pan, the crops were washed and collected, all the feet were removed and collected. When all the chickens were plucked and ready to be packaged, we would stuff each bird with a neck, a liver, a crop and two feet and they would be ready for market. We had a few stores that we supplied and as our neighbors and friends heard about our business, we sold more to them than to the shops. Our birds were huge and clean and the meat made a tasty Sunday dinner so we had no problems getting them sold.

After the harvest, Daddy would wash the floor of the coop and remove the feeders and watering containers and let the coop air out for a few days, then a visit to Seed Store, the agricultural supply center, would result in a new batch of chickens and the process would begin again.

And then there were the cows. Raising cattle requires more land than we had at our house in the housing scheme so Daddy was resourceful. Not far from our house, there was a third housing scheme project that the PNP government had planned but didn't work on before they lost power in the early 1980s. Throughout the eight year JLP term in the 1980s and early 1990s, the land was bare and so could be used by enterprising farmers who staked out a lot for their own farming purpose. There was also adjoining land that belonged to the Manning's Home (a juvenile center/ reform school for boys) and which should have been used for the boys to learn subsistence farming. However, this land, also lay idle, and Daddy could tie his cows on this land to graze. There was lots of land and a nearby tank with water to irrigate the crops and water the animals so it was a good system.

Every now and then, a cow would give birth to a calf and Daddy would milk the heifer and bring home fresh cow's milk in a little bucket. Mummy would boil it to sterilize it. I didn't like this milk at all. When it boiled, a skin formed on the top, which Mummy told me was the cream rising to the top. She told me this was proof of how rich the milk was but for me, it tasted too natural. I was used to the more watery Long-Life milk in a box but I had a lot to learn. Sometimes, Mummy would mix a little syrup into it to make it a little more palatable for me. Nevertheless, I knew it was good for me and even when I didn't want to, I drunk it up and wiped off my creamy milk moustache. Got Milk? Yes, we do!

I don't remember the butchering of the cows as vividly. These were more isolated events and they happened when I was much younger. (The cows were really bulls because cows are not usually slaughtered for meat but everybody says cows so I will keep up the trend). The "cows" were taken to my grandparents' house to be butchered and I was too young to witness the act but I know this was not something my dad did himself. He would arrange with a local butcher who would come to my grandparents' house to perform the task. Those cows weighed hundreds of pounds and hoisting the animal to the tree for the slaughter and dressing (that word again) required a complex rope and pulley system. The animal was weighed with a huge scale while it was alive and then again when it was killed.

The Health Inspector, who lived right across the road from us, would come to test the meat and they would prepare a sample for him to taste test before he would stamp the carcass with his official ink stamp so the animal could be broken down and sold. We would have beef in the fridge or deep freezer for months following this event.

The cows cost a lot more to purchase, they required so much of my Dad's effort to water and move them and they took so long to raise but he loves it. Nowadays, he doesn't butcher his cows but he raises and sells the live mature animal. He doesn't do it because it is making him wealthy, or because he needs another pastime. But even when he could have slowed down and opted for an easier life, I still think he raises the animals for the love of nature and the love of the game.

The Country's Breadbasket

Life in southern St Elizabeth communities was all about farming and everyone in my neighborhood contributed to farming in some way. Whether you tilled the soil, or raised the livestock, or drove the vans that took the produce to the supermarkets in other parishes or hotels in Negril or on the North Coast, or whether you operated the stores that sold the seeds or fertilizers or farm equipment, or worked in a restaurant that depended on a regular supply of the local produce to create tasty and convenient lunches and dinners, or sold insurance to protect the investments of those who devote their days and their nights on the farms, or whether you worked at the bank where you opened the checking accounts and gave investment loans so the farmers could operate more sustainable businesses, or whether you worked in the schools so you could teach the farmers' children to appreciate their lives and cultivate their dream of becoming anything, whether farmer or teacher or anything in between.

Or whether you were consumer - the person who drove through Southfield, on your way home from the beach or from the airport and saw the mango stall or watermelon stand or saw a vast expanse of land, rows and rows of scallion or cabbage or tomatoes, and were impressed by the straight lines with which the rows were planted, and you felt impressed to stop to buy something, to buy anything, and you got double, triple, quadruple even, of what you bought, because the kindness was so abundant and the seller just threw in some "brawta" because you smiled, or because you were traveling with your family and they gave you something special to cook for the "baby in the back seat". If that was you, then relax, and accept the accolades, because you helped support the local economy. You helped! The beauty of the breadbasket is that every person contributes to the breadbasket. Whatever their vocation, every person in my community was involved in farming. And that unity of purpose keeps my community thriving today.

Some time ago, I went to IHOP and my server was a Jamaican man. Other immigrants will identify with the fact that when you meet another person from your country, a *'yardie'*, the next question you inevitably ask each other is, "Where in Jamaica are you from?"

When the server found out I was from St Elizabeth, he asked, "Are you from Southfield?" I was taken aback, because in all the time I had been in New York, I had never had Southfield been the first guess for my hometown. Treasure Beach, or Pedro Plains even, because being beach communities, they are popular tourist destinations and therefore, are commonly known. But guessing Southfield first meant this was somebody who knew my parish and my community well. Was he from Southfield too? I immediately dismissed that as a possibility, because he didn't look familiar. It's probably not the same now, but years ago, there were only so many families in the community, and I knew most of them.

Turns out he was from Westmoreland but in Jamaica, he had spent a lot of time visiting

Southfield to play cricket. And he described in great detail the trips he and his fellow players made to Southfield, making sure they had an empty car trunk when they started their journey, because they knew they would receive gifts of fruits and vegetables and herbs and seasonings to fill it on the return trip – enough to share with their neighbors and still keep their kitchens stocked for a few weeks or until the next cricket match.

And because I had witnessed this so many times in my childhood, I couldn't help but wonder if one of those bundles of scallion and thyme or bags of carrots and cabbage and peppers or juicy watermelons, maybe came from my father's garden.

Because as I have mentioned before, food was not just given to people we knew; gifts of food were given to all who needed it or wanted it and all who could take the ministry of love with them as they continued on their journey.

Because when I was growing up, if you were a stranger passing through Southfield and the farmers knew, they would ensure you had a bag of some kind of produce to take with you so you could testify about the St Elizabeth generosity and advertise their products with your satisfaction and joy.

Sitting in IHOP, the irony of now perhaps being fed by someone to whom my parents might have given food twenty years before, wasn't lost on me.

Food

Some of my most memorable meals are Sunday dinners at Grandma's house in Yardley. Grandma liked fish but Grandpa didn't eat it. She cooked chicken for Grandpa occasionally but she didn't eat it herself. They both didn't eat curried goat. But everybody ate beef. "Beef, it's what's for dinner!" is a popular slogan of the American Beef Farmers' Industry but it could also have been the slogan for the Lloyd family Sunday dinners. We all loved it and I still do. Grandma would make this great rice and peas with red peas that were tender but whole. The rice was soft but the grains were separate. Jamaicans would describe the rice as being "shelly". There would be a whole green pepper and long strands of scallion on the top of the rice in the pot and she would scrape them aside as she served the rice. There would be thyme leaves in every spoonful and they would add to the essence to every bite. I have spent my entire cooking experience trying to imitate her rice dish. I am no closer to succeeding than when I started twenty something years ago.

Mummy would roast a piece of beef for Christmas and when we got up on Christmas morning, she would make us elegant sandwiches with crust-less bread and roast beef in gravy. Just thinking about it right now, I have to wipe the drool from my chin before it plops onto and ruins my computer. On those mornings, she would make a huge batch of hot cocoa and fill the brown teapot and we would sit on a chilly morning and drink as much "tea" as we wanted. Even though Jamaica is a tropical country, Southfield and its environs are on the Santa Cruz mountains and we get chilly mornings, especially in the Northern Hemisphere's winter months. Every morning, or sometimes late at night if we stayed up to watch TV or whenever it would rain and get cold, Mummy would offer some cocoa and we would wrap up in the living room and sip the steaming hot beverage.

When I was growing up, Mummy didn't cook chicken very often. Her specialties included more involved meals. The tripe and beans, curried goat stew and manish water I mentioned before. These all involve less tender pieces of meat and developing the juices required considerable time and effort. Even if Mom had been a stay-at-home mom, it would have been a time consuming task. But she worked full time and when we all got home in the late afternoon, she still made those delicious meals, using the pressure cooker to shorten the cook time and then allowing the stew or soup to simmer for the flavor to develop. We would get home, me tired from playing, Mummy tired from working, we would eat a snack and then go to do homework in the kitchen with the hiss of the pressure cooker providing background music. The good old days!

When Daddy cooked, the meals were different - lighter, somehow. As adults, we all have our own different cooking styles and our go-to items. Daddy's meals would be heavy on vegetable and a lighter protein – eggplant or ackee with saltfish, pickled mackerel with tomatoes, corned beef and cabbage and the pot would be full with green bananas with some of the peels to keep the bananas from turning black, slices of yellow yam, dasheen and dumplings made from a mix of flour and cornmeal. When we went to church on Sabbath, Daddy would have one of these great meals waiting for us when we got home. When he came to pick us up, we would all come home to the smells of one of those delicious vegetable-rich meals to greet us.

Mark's go-to meal is a steamed whole fish with white rice. If he came home late at night and there was no more food, you could be sure after a while you would smell the aroma of a fish being steamed in the kitchen.

I have been learning to cook my whole life. I was always watching Mummy in the kitchen, wanting to help even before I was old enough to, because I wanted to do and be everything she was when I grew up. But when I turned fourteen, my official cooking lessons began. After a short while,

Mummy allowed me to make small meals on my own. My first attempts at making rice were disastrous; I just couldn't understand how neither Mummy nor Grandma ever used a measuring cup when they cooked but it always seemed to come out perfect. My first rice meal was more like a salty and soft rice pudding but everyone was a good sport and ate it and nobody threw it away. That Christmas, I decided to bake a cake with a friend and neighbor, Tracy Rance. She lived two houses away and we were in the same class at school. Somehow, at fourteen, we thought we knew enough about cakes to make our own cake without following a recipe. What resulted was a sweet, sticky mess, stuck in the bottom of the cake pan. We use spoons to dig it out and eat it like brownies. It was delicious, even if unrecognizable, but from that day on, I realized I should ask for and follow the recipes of those who had cooked before me.

When I started fourth form at Hampton, I started taking cooking classes and tried my hand at different dishes many of which were not very palatable by the time I got home and which I didn't ever try to make again. But I learned to make a mean fried chicken and it became my favorite dish so Sunday after Sunday, especially when we had fresh chickens from Daddy's farm, Mummy and I would collaborate on a meal of rice and peas, fried chicken, potato salad, cole slaw, string beans with grated cheese and carrot juice. No matter what I learned in cooking class, and in spite of the evolution of my culinary skills over the years, this remains my favorite meal, after Mummy's curry goat, manish water and roast beef sandwiches.

Washing Clothes and other Chores

When we were growing up, Sundays were often spent at Grandma's house. Early Sunday morning, my parents would pack up the laundry basket and the detergent, maybe a couple extra pans and we would all get in the car and drive to Yardley Chase where my grandparents lived. When we were little, Mummy would wash and Daddy would help her. They would take turns at the stiff scrubbing board, a huge slab of board, that had ridges cut into it. They would lean into the pan and use the scrubbing board to rub the dirt out of the clothes. It was tough on the hands but more effective for cleaning the really dirty clothes. Then the clothes were put in rinsing water to wash out the soap. Then the white clothes were put in a bath of blue water, made by dissolving a small chunk of a solid block of blue powder. This made the clothes more luminescent so they looked whiter. The colored clothes would be put into the bath with fabric softener instead and then hung out on the clothesline to dry. There were only two clotheslines at Grandma's house and sometimes all the clothes didn't fit so we would lay socks and other items on the tank's concrete surface, the "barbecue" to dry.

When I got old enough to help with the laundry, Mummy would wash and I would rinse and hang the clothes but I still couldn't keep up with her. She would wash and sometimes when I hung an item, she would tell me to move it so it wouldn't be in the sun. Or she would show me where to put the pins so they wouldn't leave a mark.

Jackets that were hung by the area that rested on the hip, or pants that were hung by the waistband, we would double them so the clothespin would leave its mark on the inside and not on an area that would be visible when the item was being worn. I would see girls at school who had these huge pin marks on the clothes and I would know they hadn't yet learned those lessons from their moms. Even when we washed clothes at home, the lines were never enough and we would constantly monitor them so we could take the dry items inside to create more space on the lines. My uniforms and Daddy's shirts and some of Mummy's lighter colored clothes were washed early and so they would dry fast in the morning sun. In a couple hours, they were dry enough to remove from the line and we would take them inside and lay them across the bed. This would keep them from wrinkling and would ease the ironing process later. If we needed the line space before they were completely dry, we would move them so they were hung double or triple and continue to air dry while taking up minimum space.

And while we worked together, Mummy would tell me stories or I would tell her stories or Daddy would entertain us.

On the days we did laundry at our house, when we got to a certain point in the load, I would go inside to start the cleaning. When we lived at the house in the scheme, the house was small and really easy to clean. There was the verandah, the living room, two bedrooms, the bathroom and kitchen and it was all tiled with a red and white terrazzo tile. Sometimes I would start with the living room. When I started high school, they taught a class in home management and covered a section on the proper way to clean the house, the sequence in which things should be cleaned and how often they should be cleaned to keep the house tidy. I excelled in that course because by that time, Mummy had already taught me those things at home. Although she had taught me, some of those chores were not things I did regularly. Mummy was mistress of her house and although she allowed me to help with cleaning the floors and straightening the rooms on the weekend, she took care of the heavy cleaning. When I would dust, she could always use the cloth or feather duster and get things cleaner. When I would clean the floor, she would move the furniture and clean the areas behind the big settee. There was always something to learn from watching her. When we had any holidays, she would allow me to help with the special cleaning. We would use the feather duster of the broom to brush the ceilings and the walls to remove any cobwebs. She would use take a damp cloth and clean the settee, beating out the cushions and cleaning out the area under them. We would move the furniture and clean under them, first with the soap and water, then a floor

sufficient to scan the front page and the headlines but the joy of delving through the entire page, spreading the large papers open and reading one article after another, this was a Sunday evening activity. The Jamaica Observer, was introduced in the mid 1990s, its pages half the size of the Gleaner. It eventually gained popularity and market share, delivering good reporting and articles and after a while, we would buy, not one but both newspapers on Sunday mornings, sharing the sections when we read the paper in the evenings. The Observer had a different style, more entertainment articles, more colored pages, the Gleaner, more sober journalism, more conservative editorials. There was room enough for both newspapers to coexist and we learned to appreciate them both, even find them both necessary. However, it's the Gleaner that lives on in my memories.

All in the Family

My grandfather was, quite possibly, the first love of my life. I never knew my father's father because he passed away before I was born and I've never seen a photograph of him. As an adult, one night I had a very vivid dream of him –or the "him" I thought my paternal grandfather was - but it's hard to describe someone you've never met. I decided to let that dream go.

But my grandfather, the man I called Grandpa, was my mom's father, Albert Hutchinson Lloyd or Mas Hutchie to those who knew and loved him most.

Once, my aunt told me that he used to be a cross man with a quick temper. He used to drink and smoke and who knows what else. Simon, a kid who lived across the street from him, got so nervous when he was around that he would rather cross the street and run home to avoid passing my grandfather on the road. I didn't see any of those things. If he had ever been any of those things, those qualities disappeared as he mellowed into the grandfather of my memories.

Grandpa was the first person to spoil me. When I was a baby, we lived with them for a couple years while my dad completed college. I wasn't the first of his grandchildren because there were my aunt's two older children and my uncle's son and my brother but I guess I was the first of his grandchildren who lived in his house as a baby at that age and stage. Whatever the reason, he claimed me as his baby. Maybe I changed him. He definitely changed me.

He had a real sweet tooth and he always had candy of some sort in his pockets or tucked away someplace in the house. My aunt told me that when I cried as a baby, he would pound candy into cheesecloth and give it to me to suck. I started eating candy before I had teeth. Is there any wonder I am sucking on Caramel Nips right now?

When we went to visit my grandparents on Sunday mornings, Grandpa would often be away from the house in one of his many gardens, and I would scamper down the hill in the backyard to find him. When he saw me coming, he would stand and stretch out his arms so I could run into them. Although I was just a kid then, he was a strong man because my momentum did nothing to shake him. He would wrap me into a bear hug and rub his chin stubble on my cheek. Then he would put his hand in his pocket and give me a candy. There were always ginger logs, fruit logs or icy mints in his pockets. I wondered if there was a never-ending stash in his pockets, like one of those clown suits with the ribbons. Did he keep the candies on his dresser at night, stacking them in his pocket in the morning at the same time he took up his handkerchief or his keys? How did he buy these candies? Looking back, I can't recall that candy was sold in such large quantities to individuals. He would have probably requested a dollar or so worth at the shop each time. However he did it, there was always enough to share.

My family and I didn't go to church every Saturday but when we did, after Sabbath school when we went into the main sanctuary for divine service, when we established our seat in the pew on the right close to the back, I would walk over to his pew, fourth row from the front in the left,

or two rows behind the choir, aisle seat. I would walk up behind him, hoping to surprise him but he always knew I was coming. And when I sat next to him, he'd offer me a candy before I went back to sit with Mummy. It was our tradition.
Some Sundays when we were at my grandparents' house, after dinner, Grandpa would uncover "the sugar-head". The "sugar-head" was a semi-solid block of sugar, grated coconut and molasses that he would cut off in chunks and we would suck for the sheer bliss of sucking on sugar.
Grandpa had a special name for me. He called me Felicia Townsend for a reason I have yet to discover. It might have been his old love, a former teacher, a name he'd seen in the newspaper or made up. No one ever told me who this person was, if she did indeed exist. But I was Felicia Townsend to him and that was fine with me. He never called me just Felicia either. Whenever he would use the name, it would be the whole name or not at all. As a child I was a picky eater, chatting while everyone else ate so that I was the last one with food still on her plate.

Grandpa would sit with me while my brother and cousins ran off to play and he would tell me stories of his childhood. He told me about his mother, Ma Cotty, about going to England to work when he was younger, about returning to Southfield, buying land and building the house with his own hands. Later in the afternoon, he would go to the work shed and fashion toys for my brother and cousins from scrap wood. There were things he didn't tell me. He didn't talk much about some parts of his life. Like the fact that he didn't eat fish because his father had died from having a fish bone stuck in his throat. When Grandma cooked fish, she prepared something else for him to eat and she tried to get rid of the fish smell so he wouldn't have to deal with it. All my uncles would go to Jacks' Hole to fish from time to time and it wasn't often that there wouldn't be fish around but that didn't bother him. He just didn't eat it and he didn't mention it much. Mummy eventually told me that story. Occasionally, he would talk about his brothers and sisters, mentioning their names and stories of their childhood. But he was one of the last remaining of his siblings. His brother, SonSon, lived not far away and attended church with us. His sister, Renie and his brother Joe were the only others that remained and though he exchanged correspondence with his sister from time to time, they weren't a part of his day-to-day life. His brothers, Uncle Luther, Uncle David, Uncle Putt, his sister Aunt Nid, they had long passed away by then and he didn't talk much about them either.

My grandpa was quiet but firm and he tried to not let one quality outdo the other. I remember a Christmas morning when we had just gotten a bingo game set and Grandpa was playing with us in the kitchen. Uncle Johnny and Bertie, the twins, had had too much to drink, as they often did, and they were engaged in some quarrel in the backyard. My mom and Grandma had gone out to try to squelch the quarrel and get them to separate in peace and go sleep it off. But one or the other of them had gotten more rowdy than usual and was threatening some kind of violence. Grandpa didn't go out there at first, probably because he was so angry at them coming into the yard with the nonsense on Christmas morning so he stayed inside and kept us protected and occupied, playing Bingo and trying to maintain his calm demeanor. When he realized they weren't going away, he left us for a moment, went outside, broke up the scuffle and came back inside just in time for us to resume the game so I could shout my triumphant "Bingo!"

Even when his children didn't live up to their potential, he didn't harp on them. Uncle Johnny, one of his twin sons, lived at home for a long time while everyone else went to make their own way in life. He probably didn't endorse the choices Johnny made or the hours or company he kept and the things he did so he built him a room on the front of the house so they could coexist in peace. Later, he got the land surveyed and started to subdivide it. He gave Johnny the portion he would have bequeathed to him and helped him build what became known as "the ranch".

Johnny wasn't the only one to live close to home. Grandpa's eldest son, second only to my Mom, was Uncle Bobby. He lived next-door to my grandparents. His house had been built back in the 1970s when my uncle got married. Another uncle, Albert Jr, but known as Bertie, Johnny's twin, would come to stay whenever there was trouble with his girlfriend. When that relationship eventually ended, he moved back home until he could build his own version of "the ranch"

Grandpa was bald but if you only saw him casually, you might never have known because he always wore a felt hat. The only times you would see him without his hat were when he was sitting in church or in the house. He had several hats - a special hat with a feather in the band for church, an old hat for working around the yard and a semi-regular hat for the nights when he would go to the old local bar to drink sodas with his best friend, Mas John. When Grandpa quit drinking alcohol, it must have been hard to keep going out with his friend without the temptation to drink but his relationship with Mas John was important to him. They had been best friends for most of their lives, going to England together, returning to live in the same community and they never spent holidays without sharing a meal at each person's house. Grandpa was healthy and strong. He drank Ferrol for its medicinal properties without having a cold. He believed in the powers of castor oil and he swallowed a large tablespoon of the stuff every day without fail. He worked hard to provide for his family and he made time to spend with them. He was talented and handy. In his younger days, he was a carpenter and he told me stories of walking miles and miles in the morning to work on houses and then walk back home in the evenings. As a child, I remember him coming to our house to build things and seeing new construction at my grandparents' house and knowing he had built them. When they got indoor plumbing, it was from a tank he had built himself. When the outdoor kitchen got too rickety, he tore it down and built a new one closer to the main house even if the first one was only twenty feet away to begin with.

When I got sick as a child, my grandparent's house was my favorite hangout spot. And I was sick a lot with allergies of one kind or another.

My dad would joke that I probably got sick so I could go "scratch Mas Hutchie head". But when I became a teenager, I didn't spend as much time there as before. I was old enough to stay home alone if I wasn't feeling well. And our weeknight visits were more infrequent as we were often so busy with school and work responsibilities and my grandparents went to bed as soon as the news was over, so if we were going to visit we had to be in and out before 8:30 p.m.

We spent some Sundays there but there was so much going on. I never thought about how our lives were changing but I imagine my grandparents must have. They foresaw the need to pass on their traditions even as our lives were different and the world they knew was changing. I remember one day Grandpa taught me how to plait straw into a zigzag pattern. It was something I had seen him do so many times before but I had never really learned how. Grandma, it seemed was the expert at plaiting, doing complicated 15 strand and 21 strand straw patterns and rolling it into massive coils as she went. But Grandpa would often take out three broad straws and do a zigzag pattern just for fun and that day, he showed me how to start it, how to bend the straw at the right angles so it would create the pattern and how to add more straws so it could continue as long as you wanted it to. He said it was important that somebody in each generation knows how to do it so the pattern could also continue on throughout time, as long as we wanted it to. I felt like I kept the secret of the Holy Grail.

When I turned fifteen, my grandpa started getting a little sick. He'd never been sick before that I knew of. He'd lost some of his hearing and he had a hearing aid that he didn't like to wear. His being hard of hearing didn't seem to hinder him hearing everything I said to him and I didn't really think he needed the hearing-aid or at least he never showed that he did. But then he started gaining weight and it seemed only around his stomach. My mom was very concerned and she urged him to go to the doctor. He had a big stomach by the time he went to the doctor and he was told that fluid was gathering in his stomach and he would need to get it drained. He went to the hospital to get it drained and he was fine again. He looked like the man he'd been years before but it only lasted a few months before his stomach started looking bloated again. After getting it drained a second time, he started developing a shortness of breath and he was in the hospital for a couple days. We went to visit him there and I remember not liking the feeling of being in a hospital. When he asked me to sit with him, at first I was reluctant but Mummy urged me to sit on the bed with him because no matter how uncomfortable the hospital made me, I shouldn't let that affect how I interacted with Grandpa. I sat and held his hand and he smiled.

A few days later, he was back at home when grandma called that he was having the same shortness of breath. My dad went to pick him up to take him to the hospital. I remember being at home when they stopped by on their way to Mandeville, my dad driving and grandpa in the front seat. Even at his age, he was still so tall that he held his left hand out the window, his elbow on the top of the lowered glass and his fingers grasping the top of the door. He always rode like that.

I don't think I ran to greet him the way I used to run to do when I was a child but I was still so happy to see him.

I remember when I was younger and he would come say goodbye to me when we were leaving, he would whisper some nonsense statement to me and I would think about it that this was the last thing he said to me today and I would keep it in my mind until the next time I saw him. But try as I might, I cannot recall what he said to me that day except that he was going to the hospital and he'd be back.

He was in the hospital for a couple days and grandma went to visit him and said he was doing well and should be home by the weekend.

On Friday morning, Mummy and I went to Mandeville to see him. It was still too early for visiting hours so we stopped at the furniture store and bought a fancy new dresser and got some oranges to take for Grandpa. But when we got to the hospital and looked in the ward, we couldn't see him and the nurse who had just come on duty couldn't tell us where he was. We walked around confused and panicking and I remember saying to Mummy that he had probably gotten well enough and when Uncle Mackie came to visit, they had released him so he was on his way back home. I could see from the worried look on Mummy's face that she didn't share that opinion. Just then, we saw one of my parents' friends, Errol Wellington, who was visiting his wife in the hospital. Mummy told me to wait in the lobby and she went back to try to find out about Grandpa. When they came back, Mummy just held me and Mr. Wellington said the words that changed my life forever - Grandpa had passed away. I remember being stunned, like hearing a hammer strike you and knowing how much it was going to hurt even before you could feel anything. Mummy tried to hold me up but I just slid against the wall to the floor.

The face of my world had changed and nothing, yeah nothing, was ever going to be the same. From that day on, things would be remember as before Grandpa died or after Grandpa died. Everything I thought of him was going to be a memory. There would never be a new Grandpa-and-me memory to be made. Grandpa was now a part of history.

Mr. Wellington drove us back to Yardley to break the news to Grandma. She saw us get out of the van and she knew without Mummy saying a word. She had been cooking, excited at the prospect of her husband coming back home. I remember her being confused and taking the pot off the wood fire and putting it down and saying over and over to no one in particular, "What am I going to do now? Everything crash. Everything crash." And then the tears came. Grandma cried. My mom cried. I cried. Everyone from the community came and we all cried. Miss Beryl cried for Ma Hutch as she called him. Auntie Bernice came from Canada with her family and they cried. Uncle Larry came from England and he cried. Uncle Keith came from St. Ann with his family and they cried. Every time we felt that our tears had run out, we found a new well and cried some more.

My grandpa was the first person I had ever known so well and lost so suddenly and so completely. And I never got to say goodbye. I wondered if he knew how much I loved him. I wondered what were his last thoughts of me. Mummy was angry because she said if the doctors knew he was that sick, that they should have told us so he could have stayed at home and died in his house, surrounded by his family, instead of alone in a hospital bed surrounded by strangers. That really hurt her but it was too late. Nothing could help ease the loss. My grandpa was gone.

Mas John, his best friend of fifty-plus years, and from whom he had not been separated for more than a few days in that long friendship, also died exactly one month later. It seems you can, indeed, die of a broken heart.

Grandma Vera

I call her Grandma Vera here to distinguish between my two grandmothers but I never had to do that when she was around. Grandma Vera was Grandma and Grandma Kez was Grandma Kez. Grandma Kez was Daddy's Mom, she lived in Manchester and we saw her less frequently but Grandma Vera was Mummy's mother, she lived a few minutes drive away and we saw her all the time. When I was a baby, we lived with her for a while, I can't remember how long. Actually, I don't remember that period at all but I do remember spending lots of time with her when I was sick. By the time I started school, she was retired and spent most of her days at home. She worked in the house and in the garden and she was very active in the church and in the community. She had a list of people who she had sort-of adopted and whom she made rounds to take care of. There was a family that lived down the hill from her house and she would make trips to their house every few days to bring them supplies of some sort or treats for the children.

There was a little old man who lived by himself also down that hill and she would go by to make sure he had clean clothes to wear and food to eat. She took her mission work very seriously and she was always visiting neighbors to conduct Bible studies and invite them to church. She worked with the group at church to gather food and clothes for needy families and we would take our bags of used clothes for her to distribute. Sometimes, her younger daughter, Auntie Bernice would also send a barrel from Canada and she would make sure the clothes and food items got to the people who needed them most. She taught me about giving of yourself - giving of what you have received and without expecting to receive acknowledgement or anything else in return. She didn't give because she wanted something back, but she did tell me a secret, that when you give, you do get again. She said, "The more you give, the more you get". And it was true because she was always receiving and she was always giving more.

Whenever we went to her house, whether she had been expecting us or not, she always had a meal ready and treats for us. If we went there after school one afternoon after she and Grandpa had finished eating, she would have leftovers that could stretch to feed us all. It was like the feeding of the five thousand every time. And she would collect the fruits from the trees in anticipation of our visits. There were three hogberry trees in the backyard and they were all different species so each set of berries looked and tasted different. The hogberry trees bore fruit in early September to November. The trees were tall, too tall to climb and the berries were no good unless they were ripe. They were not the type of berries you picked and allowed to ripe. Instead, you would go to the tree in the early morning and collect the berries that had fallen overnight, wash them and enjoy. The tree that was directly behind the house was the best – the berries were not as sweet as the one towards the right fence but they were more plentiful, they were fatter and fleshier. It was also the more popular tree and the kids from across the street would sometimes come by to collect and eat the berries. So would my uncles who at one time or another would walk through the yard in search of the treats. When she was expecting us, Grandma would go by and collect the treats and save them so if we were not able to find anything on the ground when we visited, she had a stash for us.

There was a tamarind tree on the right side of the house and she would collect the mature fruit and make a paste with sugar. She kept it in a sealed jar and when we came, she would use a spoon or table knife to loosen some of the paste and put it in our hands for us to lick. Delicious stuff! She also added water to this paste to make a great beverage for Sunday dinners.

She had a cashew tree on the other side of the house, in the garden that separated the house from Lovers' Leap, and she would save the ripe cashew fruit for us. The fruit was "stainy" when it was just picked so it was best when it was picked and allowed to sit for a few days.

She had a safe in the inside kitchen (there were two kitchens – the one inside with the gas stove and counters and dining table and the one outside with the wood fire where she did most of the cooking and washing up). Like death, taxes and a new movie every Saturday night on HBO, it was a guarantee that Grandma always had a treat in the safe. It was a cabinet with mesh sides that Grandpa had built her. She used it to store the everyday and medium fancy dishes and to keep the treats away from ants and any other pests that would invade the kitchen. For a while, she didn't have a refrigerator and I remember she would store the condensed milk by placing it in a shallow dish filled with water and covering the top with a saucer. It kept the flies out of the top and the ants couldn't swim to get to it from the bottom. Genius.

She was a master cook and homemaker and she made it seem effortless, always, always singing or humming a hymn while she went about her daily tasks. Her house had red floors, floorboards and concrete tiles stained red with house polish and she kept it sparkling. I remember she would collect some bushes and make a broom, which she would use to sweep the house. The leaves of the " green ballad" bush, she said cleaned the tiles while it removed the dirt and she would usually have one of these brooms right outside. One of the things I remember most about Grandma's cooking was the bammies. The bammy, at first glance, might resemble a tortilla. It is white and flat as a pancake but on closer inspection, you realize that it is not a gluten based dough held together with water; rather, it is a complicated ensemble of individual pieces, held together by prayers and faith. The bammy process is long and very involved and over the years, I saw Grandma work on each stage but I was never there to see one cycle from start to finish, since it took several days to complete a batch. First, she would harvest the cassava. The cassava is a root crop and like many plants, there are different varieties. There are stringy cassava roots that are best boiled and eaten as a starchy vegetable. But the one for bammy is much more starchy, the peel is flaky and when it is cut, the inside is hard and white. Grandma would scrape the skin off and stack it in a bucket of water to preserve the white color. If the raw cassava is left, the starches would oxidize and darken.

When she would complete the peeling, she would wash them again in clean water and keep them stacked in water. She had a long grater, industrial size, about three feet long. It was a piece of metal, perhaps from a paint can, that Grandpa had flattened and cut and used a nail to pierce holes all over then nailed it to a long board. She would sit on a bench, lean the grater against her legs to start the grating. She would put a large metal bowl (the "pudding pan") at the bottom to collect the grated product and begin. The cassava root is hard and often when she was grating it, the root would slip and she would cut her hand on the grater. She would tip some of the water to wash the blood away and when it stopped, she would be grating cassava again. She did this for hours and when she was done, she would have a large, white mass, with a consistency like a thick puree. Then there were the straw sacks that were made for the purpose of draining the liquid away. They called this sack a catacoo. Or at least that is how I will spell a word I have never seen written. The catacoo was a long pouch, maybe four feet long but only about seven inches wide. The straw allowed the water to drain leaving the cassava behind. Grandma would pour the grated cassava into the catacoo and take it to the "press" under a group of trees where Grandpa had used logs to make a small bench. Here she placed the catacoo on the logs, placed some board on top of the sack and then weighed it down with several huge stones. The stones would help gravity to drain the water from the cassava and the canopy of trees helped to keep the elements at bay. Over the course of a few days, the stones would be removed and the catacoo turned and moved to ensure the process was being done evenly. At the end of that process, the cassava would be dry and mealy and Grandma would remove the sack and pour the contents in a big pan. Then she would take out the mortar and pestle and she would put a little bit at a time in the mortar and pound it. This would break out the clods and develop the starch. I remember being awestruck when she would heave the pestle and pound it into the mortar. I had never seen anything like it before and it required a kind of focused energy, dramatic and hypnotic at the same time. My grandmother was not a big woman but the energy she put into that mortar made her seem like a giant.

When the meal was developed, the baking process could begin. Baking bammies could be a day-long process in itself. It was done over a wood fire and it required a flat iron surface and a tin ring. The ring was placed on top of the iron surface and the cassava meal poured into it. Grandma would use her hand to even out the meal in the iron to form a smooth top surface. She would douse it with water and allow it to set. When it was set, she would lift the ring and then use a large wooden spatula to flip the bammy and then keep it pressed down. She only made one bammy at a time, focusing her attention on making each one a perfect item. But all bammies are not created equal. She made thin bammies that were perfect with fried fish or could be used to wrap a peg of pear (avocado) or dipped into a thick gungo soup. These were best eaten fresh. She also made thicker bammies that could be stored and heated up later by frying them in hot oil as an addition to an ackee and saltfish meal. Like most grandmothers, she was an expert cook and a lot of my memories of her are wrapped up in food.

When they were a young couple, my grandparents both lived in England for a while. Like many West Indians at that time, they went to England to work hard and earn enough money to return home and make a better life than they had had before they left. My grandparents had already started their family when they went to England so my mother and most of her siblings had spent some time living with relatives while my grandparents were overseas. When they returned and reestablished their lives in Southfield, my grandfather must have decided that he would not travel again. But my grandmother had not made that decision. Her younger daughter, Aunt Bernice, lived in Canada and Grandma would travel there to visit them, spending sometimes months at a time. She went to help when the children were born and to have an opportunity to really get to know them too. I remember the barrels that she and my aunt would ship so that a few days after she arrived with as many goodies as she could carry, there would be a barrel filled with more treats for us and food and used clothing to give to needy people.

Grandma was very social and sociable. She was known in the neighborhood and people would invite her to all kinds of functions – weddings, graduations, she was always invited. She was very conservative but she was always well dressed. Like many women in those days, her new clothes were always dressy clothes; we didn't spend money on casual wear - that came from the clothes that were no longer dressy enough to go out in. When I knew her, her hair was already white and though long in some places, it was fine and wispy so she almost never wore it out. But when she was getting ready for an event, she would go to the beauty parlor and get it relaxed or washed and set in soft pink curlers which, when removed, would leave the ends curly. However, even with this process, she would usually don one of her fancy hats to complete her outfit.

The only jewelry Grandma ever wore was a small metallic watch with a tiny face and even tinier numbers. The band was stretchy so it fit on her hand perfectly. And she wore a brooch on her fancy outfit for church.

Grandma had a beautiful voice and she almost always sang in the choir. I knew her as the Sabbath School superintendent for the Children's Division long before I knew what that job entailed. She attended every event at church that she could support, often walking the roughly 3 miles to church for morning and afternoon worship on Sabbath and the Sunday and Wednesday night meetings. Though she was small in stature, she was a fast walker and she didn't like being late because she was waiting on a ride. In fact, there are many times I recall Daddy going to pick her up to drive her somewhere and meeting her on the road because she had already started walking, because the journey would take less time if instead of him leaving our house and coming all the way to her house, that they met somewhere in the middle. Grandma and Grandpa were real Christians. They had morning and evening worship as a family everyday. Worship was at the same time and same place, whether it was just the two of them or if the house was full of visitors, whether it was a workday or a holiday. They sat in the living room and sang a hymn and prayed before and after they did their busy work.

Grandma spent a lot of her time taking care of other people, giving formal Bible studies but also doing things to show that she knew God and knew His loving character. She attended church every week even until her last day here on earth.

It was Christmas Eve, 1996. Grandma had made plans to visit her son, Uncle Keith, who lived in St Ann but at the last minute had changed her mind because no one wanted her to leave at Christmas. She had been worried about leaving us too, even for a few days, and another of her sons, Johnny, had left her feeling guilty. At the time, my cousin Lisa, Aunt Bernice's daughter lived with Grandma, the first stage in their family's plan to relocate from Canada back to Jamaica. As we often did, Lisa and I spent most of our spare time together so on Sabbath afternoon, after church, I went back to Grandma's house to have lunch with them. Grandma had baked a "toto" and I didn't want to miss out. After lunch, we decided not to go back to church for the afternoon program because Grandma had a bad headache that had been plaguing her all day but had gotten even worse. Eventually, I went home.

As the evening wore on, Uncle Bertie, who also lived with Grandma at that time, called to tell Mummy that Grandma was feeling worse so she should come so they could take her to the doctor. In the red Pontiac Sunfire, on the way to the hospital, Grandma had a stroke. A little after midnight, while they were at the hospital waiting for her to be admitted, a second stroke proved to be too much and Grandma died on Christmas Day in the same hospital where her husband had passed away just four years earlier.

At her funeral on New Years Eve, I wept until I knew that there were no more tears inside me. Afterwards, we each took a trinket from her things, something to remember Grandma by. I took a hollow ceramic chef that she had used to store her cooking spoons. But the truth was that I didn't really need anything.

I can see her house and all its contents as vividly in my mind as though I am standing right in it. I remember the red floorboards, the big beds, high off the ground with the *chimmey* pots under them that we would push aside when we played hide and seek on Sunday afternoons.

I remember her many song-books and hymnals that I would thumb through and try to sing, even. I remember her skin, the sun spots that she had amassed after years of working outside, and that she would cover up with the three-quarter length or long sleeves she would choose when she bought formal dresses.

I remember her generosity and selflessness, her devotion to her husband and her children and grandchildren, her unwavering love and acceptance, the way she offered to buy my dad a beer even though she didn't drink alcohol herself.

I remember the red felt hat that she wore most often when she went to Southfield, the "tie-head" that she used to cover her hair when she was home and the little pink sponge curlers she would put in her hair at night to give a little body to her light tresses.

I see Grandma's face in my mother's face and since I see my mother's face in my face, I expect someday when I am older, I might also see Grandma's face when I look in the mirror.

I don't need mementos. I remember my Grandma as though she was right here.

Portrait of a Father

In my opinion, a successful person is one who makes goals and is able to achieve them within established time frames. Success can be achieved in personal, professional and social capacities and may mean entirely different things to different people. For a disabled person, success might be the ability to overcome a physical handicap and participate in the society; for an athlete, success might be winning a medal in the Olympics; for a teacher, success might be coaching a child to excel in high school and win an academic scholarship to University. For my father, success was escaping the possibility of a life of poverty in a rural community and instead, earning various degrees and becoming a distinguished professor of mathematics.

My father was born as a middle child in a rural village in Manchester, Jamaica. During his childhood, his parents worked hard to provide financial and emotional support for seven children. However, despite honorable intentions, economic hardships rendered education a low priority and my father and his siblings did not attend school as regularly as they would have liked. Notwithstanding, my father and his youngest sister were able to so excel in their studies that they won the recognition of their headmaster who was able to provide scholarships for them. My father's abilities blossomed under the headmaster's tutelage and he received accolades for outstanding achievements that later provided opportunities for him to attend teacher's college, and eventually, university abroad.

Since my father saw the rewards that accompanied his hard work, he has never ceased setting goals and tackling the task of achieving them. He has risen from very humble beginnings to professional success through his thirst for knowledge. He has gained recognition from his peers by serving in various leadership capacities. In fact, he has been the most frequently elected President of his local chapter of the Lions Club

Organization because of the success of the group under his management.

I remember my dad working in the Electoral Office as they prepared for elections in Jamaica. Every few years, they would record the population demographics in the country, by collecting the census. Outside of the Kingston and Montego Bay metropolitan areas, this task was extremely challenging for a number of reasons - although there are a few slated residential areas and housing developments and housing schemes like the one in which I grew up, many Jamaican homes are built on family land in small communities. Off the main road, one can find an almost infinite number of smaller, less-travelled roads, graveled or dirt paths, which promise that there are houses ahead. How many houses will one encounter before you get to the end of that lane, one can never really predict. Furthermore, in informal communities, in the country where many of the men are self employed farmers, the women are housewives and others in the family a unique mix of entrepreneurs who are not formally employed but have "a hustle" from which they earn enough to keep them and their children fed, clothed and in school. One thing many of these Jamaicans, have in common, they are in no hurry to report their status for the tax-man to come calling.

So each road might have one or one hundred houses and whatever that number of homes or residents, there is almost certainly a much smaller number of persons willing to report in the Census. My dad signed up as a coordinator - one of the people in the area who employed and trained the persons who went into the communities to try to collect and record the information.

When it came time to prepare the voter's list, the census list was used as a guide for the number of eligible persons in any one community and my dad, again as a Electoral Office coordinator, found and trained persons who would go out in groups to find the persons who were listed on the census report, verify their identity and eligibility to vote, and photograph and fingerprint them so that a voter's identification card could be prepared. In a society where a driver's license and a passport was not commonplace, verifying someone's identity was not as easy as one would think, so the system relied on a lot of trust in family and other locals. The photographs were taken with the aid of a special Polaroid camera, which could take up to four images on any one sheet. Two photos were needed to accompany the voter registration application so the pictures would be taken two at a time and paper clipped to the multi-paged application, four or so long pages, made with carbon in between each layer to create multiple copies.

I remember the boxes and boxes of these applications that my father would drive around all reaches of the region collecting from the many groups of workers that he supervised. He would leave early in the morning with his Datsun 120Y car empty and return hours later, the car laden down with hundred of applications that had to be sorted and vetted before they could be turned in to the Regional Office.

All my family members helped to review the applications. We had to ensure that each application had been recorded properly – that the carbon had remained in the pages so the information had been pressed into each of the many pages – that the requisite two photographs were attached – that the photos were sufficiently bright and visible to appear on the ID card. Additionally, we had to make sure that each document had been signed or in the case of illiterate applicants, that each had printed his or her “mark” and that this had been appropriately witnessed, and that the fingerprints had been captured. Any application that was not complete was set aside to be returned to the responsible officers so they could try to obtain the missing information.

Months later, when the voter ID cards had been prepared and were ready for distribution, Daddy would try to get some of the same groups to work in the same areas, under the assumption that they were more familiar with the area having worked it at least once before.

Unfortunately, that wasn't always possible and

my dad would help with driving around and distributing them himself.

Later, when the party in power had called the elections, in the midst of all the "electioneering" that accompanied the voting season, many people complained about the voter's list – that their names didn't appear on it, that they had been assigned to one constituency as opposed to the other, more convenient one to which their family member or neighbor had been assigned, that their names were spelled incorrectly although they had failed to note that their voter's card carried the same incorrect spelling – when they complained, it must have been hard for Daddy not to take it personally, considering he had been involved in all the stages of the processing and had poured out so much of himself on it.

But he always took it in stride, returning over and over again to an often thankless job, where he was compensated to only a tiny fraction of his effort, he continued doing it because he has always been, and will always be, committed to

his community and his country and improving the lives of all those around him.
Above all other considerations, my father has always maintained a balanced life. He has never abandoned his family in the pursuit of his other goals and he inspires others to achieve similar success by mentoring local students. No student who ever entered his classroom has ever forgotten the lessons my father teaches. He is diligent in his tutelage, often inviting said students to our family home for as many lessons as it takes for them to excel in their examinations.

He pursues the joys of farming, rearing animals and cultivating crops even when the external conditions render such pursuits difficult. I cannot remember a time when my father didn't keep goats or cows, even when he had to walk miles to scope out a different location every day to find a new grassy area for them to graze. And when after months of tilling the soil and nursing tender seedlings out of the ground, the market undervalues the fruit of the harvest, Daddy calls it a successful crop even if he can only give the produce to his friends. And almost as soon after the reaping, he is at it again, planting a new crop to continue the cycle of life.

The trademark of a successful person is one who is able to be strengthened from adversity, overcome the obstacles that threaten his success and see his dreams materialize despite the odds. A truly successful person is also able to inspire onlookers by the mere determination to succeed. My father is a successful person.

Running

My family is my biggest inspiration. Because I live in New York, I don't see my parents often but their voices are such a constant presence in my head, I literally hear voices all the time.

The pioneer runner in my family is my dad. When I was a kid, my dad showed me a medal he won for a running event in his younger days. I don't recall the event or what his speed was but it made an impression on me and I remember thinking, "Running, I could do that!"

Turns out I couldn't do that. When I was about eight years old, I was diagnosed with a heart murmur. And technology being the way it was in the 1980s, in Jamaica, who knew what having a heart murmur entailed. So after several trips to the doctor and the pediatrician and the cardiologist for consultations and X-rays and ECGs, several trips that terrified my mom more than me because I didn't quite understand what was going on, the conclusion was that it wouldn't immediately impact my life but that there was a short list of things I should avoid and… I couldn't participate in competitive sports.

I was a bookworm and weekend tomboy who followed my brother around everywhere he would let me, and it wasn't like I was being groomed to be the next Olympian so that was ok.

When I got to high school, PE as we called gym class, back in the days when we played OUTSIDE, as in no ACTUAL gym, I had to do the requisite sports but when it came time for the annual sports day, even the girls who would try to dodge out of PE class, as teenage girls have probably always been trying to do, even those girls who didn't attend a single PE class wanted to participate in sports day so they could win medals.

Sports day was the day when the athletes would show up and show out and prove what they were made of; it was the day when the girl with the knobby knees would prove once and for all that there was power in those knees and win the long jump event, or the tall skinny girl who towered over her classmates and who didn't quite fit in with the boy-crazy group, where THAT girl would scissor over the high jump bar and make two hundred new friends immediately.

Sports Day was the day when the girls licked powdered glucose from their hands before they took off on the long-distance run, becoming instant champions on the largest stage that the 700-plus population of my rural, all-girls high school could provide.

Sports Day was the day when medals were given out and all but one of the houses that we were organized in, would concede defeat and the individual champions celebrated, their names shouted by all the members of their house as they acknowledged what those girls had done to make us all proud.

Sports Day was the day dreams were made of and I wanted more than anything, to be one of those green and yellow bedecked (the color of my house, Jackie Minott) champions, who made a victory lap around the track, feeling the love from the crowd as they applauded and cheered and shouted my name, celebrating my victory, OUR victory. Oh man, I WANTED TO RUN!

But I couldn't. It wasn't like if I DID run, that I would have won. I wasn't an athlete by any stretch of the imagination. But I also knew that I **couldn't** run and that just... well, it meant that my dream had no chance of coming true.

Which is why a couple years ago at my first physical at a new doctor, I announced before I climbed onto the table, "I have a heart murmur", so she wouldn't have to listen and listen and then try to figure out how to break the news to me gently. So she listened and checked and used some fancy equipment that in my childhood it took weeks to get an appointment to be hooked up to, then she taped some conducting pads and wires to my chest and listened and then listened some more and said, "It's just a slight murmur. You'll be fine", I almost ran down the stairs to get started with the rest of my life. I wanted to start my running life. I couldn't wait to RUN.

That's why the first medal I received for finishing a ten-mile race I did in the Bronx, is dedicated to my dad.

I don't know if I'll ever reach the levels of personal success that my parents enjoy but, "Hey, Dad, I have a medal for running now too. Thanks for motivating me and inspiring me and challenging me to RUN WRIGHT. Here's to you, Dad!"

Driving

Boys are born knowing how to drive. As children, they are given toy cars and trucks to practice until adults will give them the opportunities to drive and prove what they have always known. Parallel parking never was and never will be a challenge for boys, because boys are born knowing how to drive. Girls, on the other hand, need driving lessons.

My father had a Datsun 120Y when I was growing up. That was not his first car. He had an Escort when I was younger and at least one other car prior to me being around but my memories are of the Datsun. It was pale yellow, then white and later a reddish orange color. I remember when the format of license plate numbers changed in Jamaica and the day Daddy came home with a new plate: LN 5499.

It was a small car. By today's standards, it would be a compact car but it felt like a luxury sedan when I was growing up. The black leather seats were my mattress for so many excellent naps and sleep sessions as my dad drove us place to place across the country, pointing out interesting sites and telling us stories of place names and people he knew who lived there. He took us to each of the fourteen parishes, multiple times, for day outings and overnight trips. Together, he and my mom made sure we knew our country.

The car was a right hand drive, as Jamaicans follow the British system of driving on the left side of the road. Jamaican country roads are narrow and often winding, especially where roads have been made in treacherous mountainous regions. Sharp hairpin curves and blind corners are often the rule instead of the exception. It is not the situation in which one wants to forget even for a moment which side of the road he should be hugging.

My dad had lived for a few years in the United States when he attended college in the early 1970s and later he visited his sister, Auntie Daph, who lived in New York at the time. And when he was there for any considerable period, he would have done his driving on the right side of larger streets.

So when he returned to Jamaica, in order to keep himself in check, there was a black bumper sticker with yellow writing permanently fixed to the glove compartment in his car. "*Remember, Keep Left*".

Later when I was learning to drive my own car in Jamaica, the memory of that sticker was enough to keep me focused. Even later, when I drive in the United States and have to constantly remind myself, like Dorothy, that I am not in Jamaica anymore and the rules of the road are a little different, I call to mind that bumper sticker so I can do the opposite. Someday, I might get my own version of that bumper sticker for my own glove compartment to put my own spin on the sticker of my childhood. Mine will probably say, "*Remember, Keep Wright*"

The challenges of having a car for such a long time meant that there were times my dad needed to do repairs on his car but the parts weren't readily available and he had to wait until they were ordered. Back then, the taxi system was not as it is now. There were mini buses that plied the major routes between Southfield and Junction, and going on to Gutters, then Mandeville or Santa Cruz and so on. There was also a big market bus, the *Royal Rose* that passed on the way to Black River early in the morning and on its return trip to Manchester in the late afternoon. A later bus, *The Ambassador,* would pick up those who had missed the *Royal Rose* or had a later schedule. That was one option to getting to Black River. Mr. Facey also drove a mini-bus from Southfield to Black River and made a couple trips per day. This was the more viable option and on the days when Mummy and I took the bus to school, this was usually our transportation.

Although my parents have had a car throughout their whole relationship, my mom doesn't drive. When I was younger, my dad told me the story once that my mom used to drive but she doesn't anymore. There was an accident or near miss of some kind and she decided she'd rather be in the passenger seat than around the wheel. The fact that we only had one car growing up meant we went everywhere together or not at all and it made for great family closeness even if it wasn't always convenient for everyone. I now appreciate the wisdom of their decision.

There were days when my dad would leave his car at home and take public transportation to work and those are the days when, unbeknownst to my parents, my brother would practice his driving in the driveway. I don't remember the first day I realized this fact but I remember seeing my brother with the car at the end of the driveway, steering it back towards the house and I was so nervous because I didn't know if he could do it but he looked so calm and relaxed like this was something he had done thousands of times before. Perhaps, he had!
After this, I started to think driving was instinctive and easy.
When I turned 20 and decided it was time to buy a car, Daddy took me for a driving lesson one Sunday afternoon. I was so nervous that holding the wheel was almost impossible. My brother, by that time the proud owner of the same Datsun

120Y, a gift from Daddy when he traded up to the white Toyota Corolla, also took me for lessons. I was frustrated that driving didn't seem to come as naturally to me as it had to him and I kept stalling the car. I decided to pay Mr. Witter, a driving instructor, for a couple lessons. On the day of the first lesson, as I stood outside my job waiting for him to show up, I realized the sky had never looked as dark as I saw it. When he arrived, the first raindrops had begun to fall. He said, "It's going to rain. Do you still want to go for you first lesson today?"

I muscled up, mustered all my courage and said, "Sure. It's going to be raining at some point when I am driving. I might as well learn how to drive in the rain now."

I got in and it started to pour. It rained and rained and I drove. Through puddles and around potholes, I drove. Mr. Witter complimented me on how well I handled the car. He kept asking what I drove before because he said I didn't act nervous like a beginner.

It wasn't until we got back in the housing scheme and I was about fifty yards from home that I stalled the car. And then, despite my best efforts, I stalled it again and yet again before I got to the gate. I was so happy to be home, I decided to forgo the second lesson and ask my brother to keep teaching me.

A few months later, I bought my own Toyota Corolla automatic and my brother was only too happy to teach me to drive my own car so he could preserve his transmission. I learned to integrate the conservative driving style of my dad and the less-conservative but equally as careful style of my brother and finally emerged with my own particular brand of driving. I remember the day my dad finally sat in my car as a passenger, albeit for a very short ride but he was comfortable and he had only compliments for me. Mummy and I would take longer trips on weekends, to church, to parks and to events, and she sat as calm as she does when other, more experienced drivers are behind the wheel.

Both my father and my brother continue to buy cars with standard transmission. They say it's easier to handle and you get better mileage. They say engaging the clutch and "gearing down" is the only real way to experience driving. The list of attributes is endless.

I still drive an automatic car when I can.

ABOUT THE AUTHOR

Karen received a Bachelors and a Masters Degree in Chemical Engineering, but her true passion is writing. She grew up in Jamaica and now lives in New York City. She enjoys running, biking and traveling to nature preserves for hiking and camping.

Karen maintains a blog at RUNWRIGHT.NET and does freelance writing for various magazines and online publications.

Follow Karen via:-

Blog: http://runwright.net/

Facebook: www.facebook.com/karen.wright.5876

Twitter: @kamari2001

www.ingramcontent.com/pod-product-compliance
Ingram Content Group UK Ltd.
Pitfield, Milton Keynes, MK11 3LW, UK
UKHW041939190726
13854UKWH00004B/1677